WAR STORIES

SPECIAL FORCES

Brian Williams

www.raintreepublishers.co.uk
Visit our website to find out more information about Raintree books.

To order:
☎ Phone 0845 6044371
🖷 Fax +44 (0) 1865 312263
🖳 Email myorders@raintreepublishers.co.uk

Customers from outside the UK please telephone +44 1865 312262

Raintree is an imprint of Capstone Global Library Limited, a company incorporated in England and Wales having its registered office at 7 Pilgrim Street, London, EC4V 6LB – Registered company number: 6695582

Text © Capstone Global Library Limited 2011
First published in hardback in 2011
The moral rights of the proprietor have been asserted.

Edited by Louise Galpine and Vaarunika Dharmapala
Designed by Clare Webber and Steve Mead
Original illustrations © Capstone Global Library Ltd 2011
Illustrated by KJA-Artists.com
Picture research by Elizabeth Alexander
Originated by Capstone Global Library Ltd
Printed and bound in China by Leo Paper Products Ltd

ISBN 978 1 406 22198 5 (hardback)
15 14 13 12 11
10 9 8 7 6 5 4 3 2 1

British Library Cataloguing in Publication Data
Williams, Brian.
Special forces. – (War stories)
356.1'6-dc22
A full catalogue record for this book is available from the British Library.

Acknowledgements
We would like to thank the following for permission to reproduce photographs: Corbis pp. **5** (© Louie Psihoyos), **6** (Bettmann), **8–9** (© Mathew B. Brady Studio), **11** (© Hulton-Deutsch Collection), **16** (© Peter Turnley), **20** (© Aero Graphics, Inc.), **22** (© STRINGER/AFGHANISTAN/Reuters), **27** (© STR/epa); Getty Images pp. **10** (Roger Viollet), **13** (Keystone), **15** (STF/AFP); Photo courtesy of the US Army p. **25** (Tisha Johnson, Fort Leavenworth Lamp); Rex Features p. **18**; Shutterstock **background design and features** (© oriontrail).

Cover photograph of Russian special police servicemen assaulting a building during a police show at a training base outside Moscow on 10 May 2007, reproduced with permission of Getty Images (Adel Brard/AFP).

We would like to thank John Allen Williams for his invaluable help in the preparation of this book.

Every effort has been made to contact copyright holders of material reproduced in this book. Any omissions will be rectified in subsequent printings if notice is given to the publisher.

CONTENTS

Words appearing in the text in bold, like this, are explained in the glossary.

Look out for these boxes:

WHAT WOULD YOU DO?
Imagine what it would be like to make difficult choices in wartime.

REMEMBERING BRAVERY
Find out about the ways in which we remember courageous acts today.

NUMBER CRUNCHING
Learn the facts and figures about wars and battles.

SECRET HEROES
Find out about the brave individuals who didn't make it into the history books.

INTRODUCTION

It is night. Hidden by trees, soldiers strip off their armour and strap swords across their backs. They slip into the river, and start to swim. They can see tents and fires. They are about to raid an enemy camp.

Two thousand years ago, the ancient Romans had special forces for surprise attacks such as this. Today, special forces are still the world's secret soldiers.

Who are the special forces?

Special forces in World War I (1914–1918) included Thomas Edward Lawrence, also known as Lawrence of Arabia, and his Arab soldiers. In World War II (1939–1945), British Commandos, US Army Rangers, and jungle-fighters like Merrill's Marauders and the Chindits were admired for their toughness. Modern special forces include the US Navy **SEALs**, US Army Rangers and Delta Force, US Marine Corps Force Recon, and the British **SAS**.

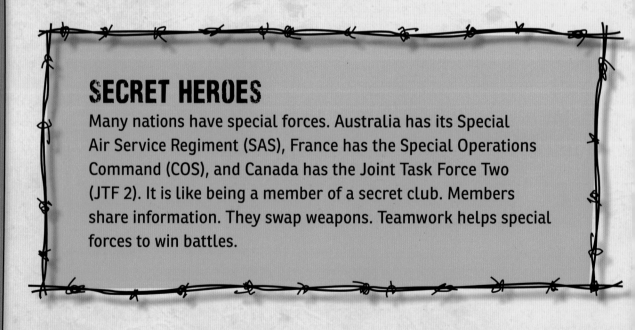

SECRET HEROES

Many nations have special forces. Australia has its Special Air Service Regiment (SAS), France has the Special Operations Command (COS), and Canada has the Joint Task Force Two (JTF 2). It is like being a member of a secret club. Members share information. They swap weapons. Teamwork helps special forces to win battles.

Special missions

Only the best people are chosen for special forces. Tough training prepares soldiers for special ops (operations and missions). Special forces gather information, destroy secret bases, hunt terrorists, rescue hostages, and train local troops for special ops.

Special methods

Special forces use all sorts of weapons, from **missiles** to bits of wire. They are very fit. Most are good swimmers, runners, and climbers. They know how to camp, how to hunt animals for food, and how to survive in forests and mountains. When on a mission, they may dress like the local people to avoid attracting attention. On the television news, they keep their faces hidden.

▼ Special forces train to fight anywhere in the world.

MOSBY'S RAIDERS

Special forces often fight differently from other soldiers. The American **Civil War** of 1861–1865 was fought between the **Union** (the northern states) and the **Confederates** (some southern states). Both had large armies, but each side also sent special forces to raid the other.

Raids and chases

In April 1862, the Union sent James Andrews and 21 other men to steal a railroad locomotive (steam train) in the south. After a dramatic chase, Andrews was caught.

The Confederates sent **cavalry** into Union territory. One such Confederate raider was General Nathan B. Forrest. Another was Colonel John Mosby, whose rangers were known as Mosby's Raiders.

▶ This is Colonel John Mosby, posing for a studio photograph.

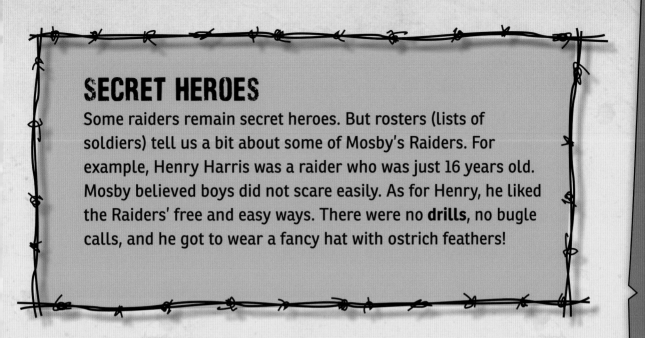

SECRET HEROES

Some raiders remain secret heroes. But rosters (lists of soldiers) tell us a bit about some of Mosby's Raiders. For example, Henry Harris was a raider who was just 16 years old. Mosby believed boys did not scare easily. As for Henry, he liked the Raiders' free and easy ways. There were no **drills**, no bugle calls, and he got to wear a fancy hat with ostrich feathers!

Mosby's most daring raid

Mosby made his most daring raid in 1863. On 9 March that year, 30 Rangers in grey uniforms rode through the night. Mosby's men all rode well. The horsemen moved like ghosts through the Virginia countryside as they carried out raids behind Union lines. They knew every trail. When Union soldiers chased them, they seemed to disappear. In fact, they usually went back home to their farms.

On that March night in 1863, Mosby led his Raiders to Fairfax Court House in Virginia. It was a small town, held by Union soldiers. The Raiders moved in without a sound. They cut the **telegraph** wires, so Union soldiers could not call for help. Then they headed for the house where they had been told Union General Edwin H. Stoughton had his headquarters.

After silencing the guards, the Raiders crept inside. The general was asleep, so Mosby poked him to wake him up. Then they hustled their startled prisoner outside. The Raiders rode away, taking 33 prisoners and 58 horses.

Why hit-and-run often won

Henry Harris, like all the Raiders, had two Colt .44 pistols. These pistols were better than swords and rifles for hit-and-run battles.

Mosby told Henry, "Don't shoot until you have something to shoot at." Each rider had two horses so that he could switch horses when one got tired. If they had to run for it, they hid out with friends. Once Walter Franklin hid behind a china cabinet while Union troops searched his girlfriend's house!

Mosby and his Raiders went on raiding until the Civil War ended in April 1865. Then they went home for good.

REMEMBERING BRAVERY

Books and magazines made Mosby famous. *Harper's Weekly* magazine called Mosby's Raiders "citizens by day, soldiers by night". Mosby wrote two books about his adventures. He later went into the law and politics, and died in 1916.

◄ This photograph shows Union officers and soldiers at their camp during the American Civil War.

SPECIAL FORCES IN WORLD WAR II

During World War II (1939–1945) German **Nazi** forces invaded western Europe, while Japan attacked parts of Asia. Special forces fought secret battles in the deserts of North Africa, the jungles of Asia, and across Europe. This secret war became more important as 6 June 1944 approached. This day was known as D-Day, when the **Allies** planned to land an army in France to defeat the Nazis.

What was the Resistance?

The Nazis invaded France in 1940. The Allies hit back, with help from the French Resistance. The Resistance was made up of people who were against the Nazi invasion. Some people fought back in small ways. They would change a road sign to send German trucks the wrong way, or make a factory machine break down. Others ambushed German soldiers and blew up railways. The Germans shot anyone who helped the Resistance.

▶ This photograph shows some French fighters preparing to attack the Nazis.

Violette Szabo

The Allies sent special forces to help the Resistance. Britain's Special Operations Executive (SOE) needed secret agents who spoke French. Violette Szabo's mother was French and Violette's French husband had been killed at the battle of Alamein, in North Africa, in 1942. Violette had a baby daughter, but now she wanted to fight. In 1943 she joined the SOE.

Training was hard. Violette learned to operate a radio, to blow up a road, and to shoot. Her instructor, Commando Les Fernandez, taught her well. Violette was soon the best shot in her class, and in 1944 she went to France.

▼ Women all over the world trained to be able to fight the Nazis and defend their countries. These women from Hawaii are learning to shoot.

Battle in France

SOE agents flew to France in small planes that could land in a field. They were also dropped by parachute. They were given false names and fake identity papers. The Nazis were on the lookout for anyone suspicious.

Violette's first mission was in April 1944. She landed in France by parachute. She was stopped by the French police but managed to talk her way out of trouble. She was soon back in England.

On 8 June 1944, two days after D-Day, she parachuted again into France. The Allies had landed and battles were raging in northern France. The Nazis were hunting all Resistance and SOE agents. On 10 June, German soldiers trapped Violette and a Resistance leader named Jacques Dufour in a house. Violette fought them off so that Dufour could escape. She kept shooting until her gun was empty.

Captured!

The Nazi secret police kept Violette alone in a prison cell. They tortured her but she would not betray friends like Dufour and Fernandez (now in France, blowing up roads). When she would not talk, the Nazis sent her to a **concentration camp** in Germany. They shot her in 1945, aged just 23.

REMEMBERING BRAVERY

Violette Szabo was given a posthumous (after death) George Cross medal for her courage. King George VI of Great Britain gave the medal to her daughter Tania after the war. In 1958, Violette's story was made into a film called *Carve Her Name with Pride*.

▲ This photograph of Violette Szabo
was taken during the war.

Sand from a French beach

Other special forces were also active in France weeks before soldiers landed there on D-Day. One May night, a US Navy **torpedo** boat sailed across the English Channel. Three men paddled ashore in a rubber dinghy, landing on a beach in Normandy, northern France. They sneaked in under the noses of German sentries – to collect buckets of sand.

Commander John D. Bulkeley did not know why he was assigned to collect sand. If captured, his story was that his men were looking for Allied pilots who had been shot down. Bulkeley knew the Germans might shoot them as spies.

The men scooped sand into their buckets. Then a light flashed. Bulkeley saw a German helmet. He flung sand into the enemy soldier's face, then used his training to kill him. The three Americans hurried back to their boat.

The mystery solved

Back in England, they handed in their buckets. The sand was taken away. What could it mean? Bulkeley finally understood after 6 June. Their beach, code-named Utah, was one of five D-Day landing beaches. The Allied generals were worried about Utah. Was it too soggy to land tanks? Bulkeley and his men had answered that question. The sand was firm.

REMEMBERING BRAVERY

Visitors travel to Normandy to see the war cemeteries, which contain thousands of graves. The many men who died there are remembered and honoured by these visitors.

▲ These American soldiers are going ashore at Utah beach on D-Day.

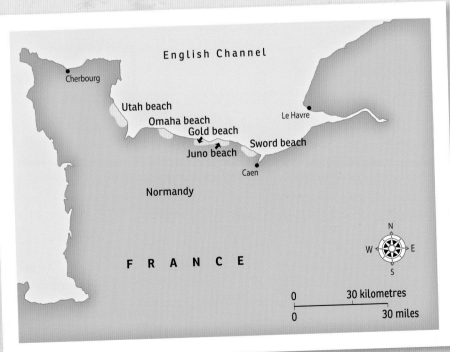

English Channel

Cherbourg

Utah beach

Omaha beach

Gold beach

Juno beach

Le Havre

Sword beach

Caen

Normandy

F R A N C E

N
W   E
S

0   30 kilometres
0   30 miles

◄ This map shows
the five D-Day
landing beaches
in Normandy,
France.

BRAVO TWO ZERO'S DESERT MISSION

Bravo Two Zero was the call sign (code or password used for radio calls) of a British **SAS** patrol in the 1991 Gulf War. This war was fought in Iraq and Kuwait, countries that are mostly desert.

Desert warfare

During World War I, Lawrence of Arabia rode camels through the desert. In World War II, a British SAS soldier named David Stirling used jeeps. Modern special forces in the Middle East use helicopters as well as trucks, but sometimes they must walk.

The war in Iraq

In 1991, **United Nations** forces went to war to stop Iraq taking over its neighbour, Kuwait. Before the main attacks began, SAS soldiers flew secretly into Iraq. Eight men of the Bravo Two Zero team landed from a Chinook helicopter on 23 January 1991. They were in enemy territory.

A mission goes wrong

Led by Sergeant Andy McNab (whose real name is Steven Mitchell), the team's mission was to watch roads, locate **missile** sites, and blow up phone lines.

Things soon went wrong. They were in the wrong place. There were hundreds of Iraqi soldiers shooting at them. The radios did not work, though they managed to send an emergency signal. It was very cold, wet, and starting to snow.

The mission was over. How were they to get home?

NUMBER CRUNCHING

Each special forces soldier carries at least 45 kilograms (100 pounds) of equipment. SAS soldiers carry rifles, machine guns, rockets, and **grenades**, as well as food, water, medical kit, and radios.

◀ Helicopters like this Chinook fly special forces in and out of enemy territory.

Trying to get home

The SAS soldiers set out walking towards Syria, which was more than 160 kilometres (100 miles) away. They soon became separated. McNab was with a group of four men, and Chris Ryan (whose real name is Colin Armstrong) was with two others. Their heavy equipment slowed them down, despite their fitness. One member of the team named Vince Phillips died from cold and exhaustion. Another was captured by Iraqi soldiers.

▲ This is Vince Phillips, who died on 25 January 1991 while on mission in Iraq.

Telling tales

Some special forces soldiers never tell their secrets. However, the Bravo Two Zero soldiers used pseudonyms (false names) to write their stories. McNab, Ryan, and a third soldier, whose pseudonym is Mike Coburn, wrote bestselling books. *Bravo Two Zero* became a film, and Ryan wrote the Alpha Force action-books for younger readers.

McNab's group stopped a car, tied up the driver and passengers, and drove off. But when they came to an Iraqi army checkpoint, they had to get out and run. After this, things got worse. A second soldier died from the cold. Another was killed by Iraqi soldiers. While trying to cross the Euphrates River, the last three were captured. The four captives were held prisoner until the Gulf War ended in March 1991. Only Ryan made it to Syria, walking all the way.

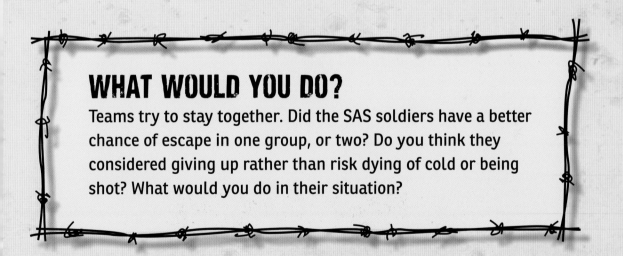

WHAT WOULD YOU DO?

Teams try to stay together. Did the SAS soldiers have a better chance of escape in one group, or two? Do you think they considered giving up rather than risk dying of cold or being shot? What would you do in their situation?

FIGHTING THE TALIBAN

Bravo Two Zero's experience showed that things do not always go to plan. All special forces soldiers are trained to work as a team, and to expect surprises. Yet, even the best trained soldier may end up alone and in danger. This is what happened to US Navy **SEAL** (Sea, Air, and Land) team member Marcus Luttrell while he was in Afghanistan.

What do SEALs do?

The US Navy SEALs are among the best special forces in the world. They fight anywhere but, being sailors, they often come and go by water. Marcus Luttrell's war, however, took him to Afghanistan, a country with no sea coast, and not much water of any kind. Here the enemy were the **Taliban** and **al-Qaeda** terrorists led by Osama bin Laden.

▼ This US Spectre gunship is one type of plane used in Afghanistan.

Fighting the Taliban

The war in Afghanistan started in October 2001, in reponse to the terrorist attacks of 11 September on the United States. Al-Qaeda carried out the attacks and the Taliban government in Afghanistan sheltered them. US and **Nato** forces went into Afghanistan to remove the Taliban government.

Special forces teams hunted in mountain caves to find Osama bin Laden. Bin Laden got away, but the Taliban government soon fell. Taliban fighters continued to fight and the war is still going on in Afghanistan.

◀ This map shows Afghanistan and its neighbours.

Hunting Sharmak

In June 2005, a four-man team of US Navy SEALs landed from a helicopter in the mountains of Afghanistan. They were on a hunting mission. Their target was a Taliban leader named Sharmak. One of the four was Marcus Luttrell. The mission was about to test him to the limit.

What was it like in the mountains?

The Americans had food and water to last several days. To help them find their way at night, they had **night-vision goggles** and a **GPS satnav** kit. The Afghanistan mountains were, Luttrell said later, "absolutely horrible". It was dark, raining, and freezing cold there. One slip and they could tumble hundreds of metres down over the rocks.

▼ These Taliban fighters are training for war.

Seen by the enemy

They scrambled on, trying not to be seen. Near a village, they ran into three Afghans with a herd of goats. They let the Afghans go, and the goat-herders quickly raised the alarm. Soon Taliban fighters turned up. Sharmak was now the hunter, not the hunted.

Battle begins

A fierce battle began. There were four Americans against fifty to a hundred Taliban fighters. Trying to find cover, Marcus Luttrell and the team leader Mike Murphy slid down the mountain, losing most of their supplies and their radio on the way. The other two SEALs followed, with the Taliban fighters chasing them. The SEALS kept firing and falling.

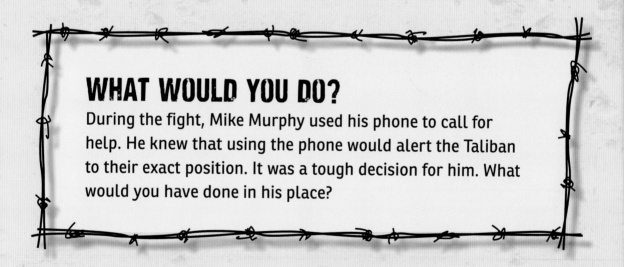

WHAT WOULD YOU DO?

During the fight, Mike Murphy used his phone to call for help. He knew that using the phone would alert the Taliban to their exact position. It was a tough decision for him. What would you have done in his place?

Left alone

The Taliban fighters were shooting from above and bullets flew everywhere. All four Americans were wounded. The enemy closed in. Murphy and his team members Matthew Axelson and Danny Dietz were killed. Marcus Luttrell was left alone.

A rescue fails

A Taliban **grenade** blew the wounded Luttrell over a cliff. The blast blew off his trousers. He had lost his medical supplies, maps, and compass. He still had his rifle, and could see and hear the Taliban hunting for him.

A US rescue helicopter flew in, but a Taliban rocket-propelled grenade sent it crashing down in flames. The crew were killed. Luttrell was too far away to see the crash, but he could see other planes looking for him.

Safe in a village

Pursued by the Taliban, the lone SEAL stumbled on, until he came to a village. This time he was lucky. The villagers hated the Taliban so they gave him shelter, looked after his wounds, and fed him. It was their custom to help a stranger in trouble.

Luttrell became friends with an Afghan policeman named Gulab. Even when the Taliban came looking for Luttrell, Gulab and the other villagers refused to hand over the wounded American.

Luttrell was finally rescued by Afghan special forces and US Rangers. A helicopter flew him and Gulab to safety. Back in the United States, Luttrell received a hero's welcome. When he was finally fit again, he rejoined the SEALs.

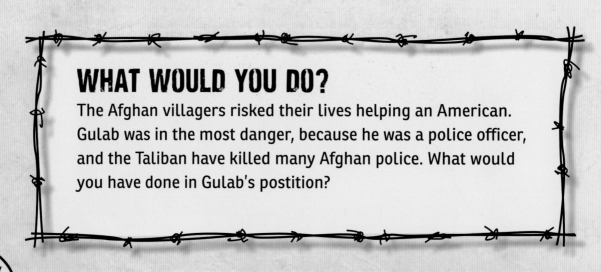

WHAT WOULD YOU DO?

The Afghan villagers risked their lives helping an American. Gulab was in the most danger, because he was a police officer, and the Taliban have killed many Afghan police. What would you have done in Gulab's postition?

▲ Marcus Luttrell was a hero when
he returned home. Here he is receiving
a medal for his bravery.

CONCLUSION

Special forces fight in dangerous war zones around the world. Most of their missions are secret. Some special forces soldiers are inspired by stories of citizen-soldiers like Mosby's Raiders. Others find inspiration from soldiers such as Lawrence of Arabia.

Lawrence of Arabia

T. E. Lawrence first went to Arabia to study castles. When World War I began in 1914, he led Arab fighters in desert raids against the Turks. Lawrence became a hero. He later joined the Royal Air Force under a false name. No one knew he was Lawrence of Arabia. He died after a motorbike crash in 1935.

REMEMBERING BRAVERY

T. E. Lawrence was a scholar who looked like a comic-book hero. He rode a camel and wore flowing Arab clothes. Yet, after the war, he avoided fame and changed his name. People read his book, *Seven Pillars of Wisdom*. Long after he died, his story was told in the film *Lawrence of Arabia*.

▶ These special forces commandos are from India's Force One. They are training to catch terrorists.

What do special forces do today?

Today, special forces work in small groups alongside other soldiers. They choose their own weapons and use hi-tech gear. Because much of what they do is secret, the men and women of the special forces are rarely identified in news reports. Their faces are blanked-out. Their names are changed. Most remain secret soldiers.

SPECIAL FORCES AROUND THE WORLD

USA

During the American **Civil War** (1861–1865), bands of raiders rode behind enemy lines. The most daring were Mosby's Raiders.

FRANCE
During World War II, special forces such as Violette Szabo and her friends, helped the Resistance in France. Special forces also helped make the D-Day landings in 1944 a success.

AFGHANISTAN
The war against the **Taliban** began in 2001, and in 2010 is still going on. Special forces went in, often by helicopter, to fight the Taliban in the mountains.

IRAQ
The Gulf War of 1991 was fought against Saddam Hussein's Iraq. Special forces teams went into Iraq before the army did, but things did not always go to plan.

SYRIA, IRAQ, SAUDI ARABIA
Lawrence of Arabia led a special forces operation during World War I. Arabia was a vast region that included modern Syria, Iraq, and Saudi Arabia.

GLOSSARY

Allies/Allied nations fighting together during World War II, including the United States and United Kingdom

al-Qaeda terrorist group founded in the late 1980s by Osama bin Laden

cavalry soldiers on horses

civil war war between different groups of people in the same country

concentration camp prison camp in which the Nazis held people under terrible conditions, until they died or were killed

Confederate one of the southern states in the United States that wanted to break away and form their own government in the 1800s

drill military training involving marching and weapon handling

GPS satnav system that shows you where you are on a digital map, using data from satellites and computers

grenade small bomb, which is either thrown or fired from a rifle

missile rocket weapon

Nato (North Atlantic Treaty Organization) 28 nations that have agreed to defend each other militarily in the event of attack

Nazi ruling party of Germany from 1933 to 1945, or a member of it. The Nazis were led by Adolf Hitler.

night-vision goggles special glasses for seeing in the dark

SAS British army regiment that is specially trained to undertake dangerous secret operations

SEAL (Sea, Air, and Land). SEALs fight anywhere and are among the best special forces in the world.

Taliban group who ruled Afghanistan until removed from power in 2001. Members of the Taliban continue to fight in Afghanistan.

telegraph system of sending messages using electricity and wires, invented in the 1800s

torpedo bomb that moves quickly under water and explodes when it hits its target

Union states that made up the United States after some southern states tried to set up their own government in the 1800s

United Nations international organization representing nearly all of the world's countries

FIND OUT MORE

Books
Non-fiction

The Who's Who of: World War II, Clive Gifford (Wayland, 2009)

The World at War – World War II: Life as a Combat Soldier, Brian Williams (Heinemann Library, 2006)

Timelines: The War in Afghanistan, Brian Williams (Franklin Watts, 2010)

Usborne True Stories: True Stories of D-Day, Henry Brook (Usborne, 2008)

Fiction

Alpha Force: Survival, Chris Ryan (Red Fox, 2004)

Alpha Force: Hostage, Chris Ryan (Red Fox, 2004)

Websites
www.violette-szabo-museum.co.uk
This website has lots of information about Violette Szabo.

www.spartacus.schoolnet.co.uk
Find out all about World War I and World War II on this website.

www.eliteukforces.info
This website can help you learn about the SAS and other British special forces.

www.sealchallenge.navy.mil
The official US Navy website can tell you all about the SEALs.

A place to visit
The Imperial War Museum
Lambeth Road
London
SE1 6HZ
www.iwm.org.uk

Visit the Imperial War Museum to learn more about the wars discussed in this book.

INDEX